SERVICE DOG

A Crabtree Branches Book

B. Keith Davidson

School-to-Home Support for Caregivers and Teachers

This high-interest book is designed to motivate striving students with engaging topics while building fluency, vocabulary, and an interest in reading. Here are a few questions and activities to help the reader build upon his or her comprehension skills.

Before Reading:

- *What do I think this book is about?*
- *What do I know about this topic?*
- *What do I want to learn about this topic?*
- *Why am I reading this book?*

During Reading:

- *I wonder why...*
- *I'm curious to know...*
- *How is this like something I already know?*
- *What have I learned so far?*

After Reading:

- *What was the author trying to teach me?*
- *What are some details?*
- *How did the photographs and captions help me understand more?*
- *Read the book again and look for the vocabulary words.*
- *What questions do I still have?*

Extension Activities:

- *What was your favorite part of the book? Write a paragraph on it.*
- *Draw a picture of your favorite thing you learned from the book.*

TABLE OF CONTENTS

What Makes a Dog a Service Dog?

A service dog is any dog that performs a job or a task that helps a person who has a physical or mental **disability**.

These tasks can be anything from guiding people down a sidewalk to sniffing out changes in a person's health.

Great Dane

Chihuahua

Any dog can be a service dog—from a giant Great Dane to a tiny Chihuahua.

How Can I Tell if a Dog is a Service Dog?

People often recognize service dogs by the vests some wear. However, service dogs are not the only dogs that wear vests. So do therapy dogs and courthouse dogs.

There are also service dogs that don't wear vests. Hearing dogs and medical alert dogs don't always need to wear them.

FACT Many hearing dogs have special leashes, capes, or jackets instead of vests.

So, how can you tell if a dog is a service dog? Take a look. Is the dog performing any tasks or helping a person who has a disability? Is the dog calm and focused on its **handler**?

If the answer to both is yes, the dog is a service dog. However, it is important to remember that it is not always possible to see that a person has a disability.

More than 80 million Americans use some type of service dog.

Serving in the Community

Many people think dogs are cute and playful, but service dogs have jobs to do. Service dogs help their handlers live and work safely. Do not pet or distract a service dog while it is working.

Distracting a service dog can be extremely dangerous to the person that needs that dog's help.

FACT Service dogs are not only trained to listen to commands, but to refuse unsafe commands.

Types of Service Dogs

Guide Dogs

Guide dogs help people who are completely or **partially** blind find their way. They are also known as seeing-eye dogs. These service dogs were first used in Germany in the early 1900s, after many soldiers were blinded during World War I.

Many of the first guide dogs were German shepherds. Today, however, breeders mostly choose golden or Labrador retrievers.

Guide dogs and their handlers work together to navigate from place to place.

Hearing Dogs

Hearing dogs use their ears to help people who are deaf or hard-of-hearing. These dogs listen for things such as fire alarms, cooking timers, crying children, and doorbells.

If there's an emergency alert going off, hearing dogs let their owners know about the danger. A hearing dog can be any breed, as long as it is intelligent and focused.

Hearing dogs don't bark to get attention. Instead, they are trained to alert their handlers physically. They may nudge the person with their nose, lick them, or touch them with their paws.

Mobility Dogs

Mobility dogs are service animals trained to help people move. They do not guide their handlers like guide dogs. Instead, they help people balance and walk from place to place. They are normally bigger breeds like the Saint Bernard or the Great Dane. This is because people often lean on them.

Some mobility dogs assist people who use wheelchairs. These dogs fetch things and help people in wheelchairs get around.

FACT Mobility dogs can open fridges, carry groceries, and perform a full range of daily tasks.

Medical Alert Dogs

Medical alert dogs warn of oncoming medical issues such as seizures or changes in blood sugar. These dogs notice slight changes in their handler's bodies, and then spring into action to alert them before a medical problem happens. They help their humans avoid serious injury and even death.

Some medical alert dogs are used by people who have severe allergies. They sniff out any **allergens** to see if it is safe for their owner to do certain things, such as going into a room, using a public computer, or eating a restaurant meal.

Medical alert dogs can smell traces of allergens and warn their handlers.

Medical alert dogs can be trained to warn their handlers in various ways, such as pawing, nudging, or barking.

Seizure dogs are medical alert dogs that can detect chemical changes in their handlers' bodies. They sense seizures minutes before they happen and alert their handlers.

Psychiatric Service Dogs

These service dogs help people with mental health conditions. They may remove possible **triggers** from an environment or alert people that panic attacks are coming.

Psychiatric service dogs can also remind people about medication and interrupt repetitive or harmful **behaviors**. These dogs need to be calm and attentive. The breed does not matter.

Psychiatric service dogs can turn on lights and enter a room first to help calm a person's anxiety.

Picking the Perfect Puppy

Trainers look for calm puppies to become service dogs. A future service dog should be alert and eager to please its handler.

Service dogs need to be at least 6 months old to start working at their jobs.

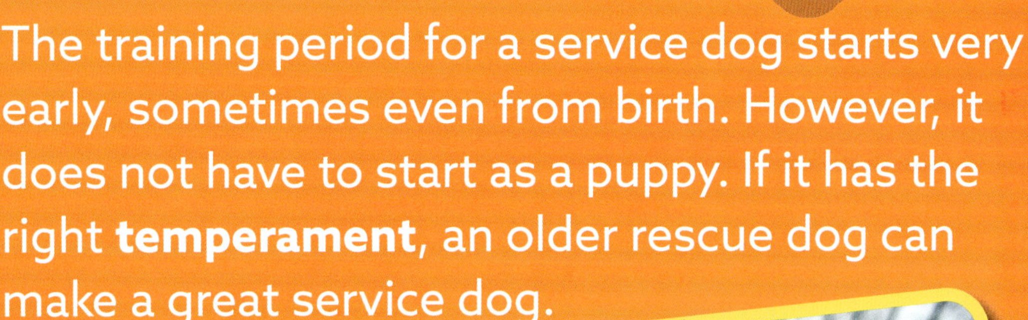

The training period for a service dog starts very early, sometimes even from birth. However, it does not have to start as a puppy. If it has the right **temperament**, an older rescue dog can make a great service dog.

Training

Service dogs can be trained by anyone, but most service dogs are trained by professionals who have completed courses and have earned a certificate.

Training one service dog can cost over $25,000. The cost depends on the job that they will do for their handler.

The average service dog needs at least 120 hours of training and 30 hours of practice in public.

Service Dogs Are Heroes

Service Dogs Help Veterans!

The first service dogs were used to help the **veterans** of World War I who had lost their sight. Today, they still help veterans returning from war.

Service dogs help veterans deal with **PTSD**, hearing loss, and mobility issues.

Service dogs can wake a person having a bad dream and help to calm them down.

Service Dogs Are Lifelines

Service dogs are carefully paired with their handlers. They share deep bonds and depend on each other.

A service dog can be trained to carry a portable phone to its owner in an emergency.

Service dogs are lifelines for their owners. They help keep them safe and allow them to live more independent lives.

Glossary

allergens (al-UR-jenz): substances that cause allergic reactions in people

behaviors (bi-HAYV-yuhrz): things that people or animals do

disability (diss-UH-bil-uh-tee): a condition, either mental or physical, that prevents a person from performing one or more tasks in their everyday life

handlers (hand-duhl-erz): people who own and use service dogs

partially (PAR-shuhl-ee): not completely, or only having part of something (i.e., partially blind means the person has some sight)

PTSD: stands for Post-Traumatic Stress Disorder, a mental health condition that affects people who have lived through difficult and shocking events

temperament (TEM-pur-uh-muhnt): a person or animal's nature, especially how they act or respond

triggers (TRIG-urz): to cause something to happen

veterans (VET-ur-uhnz): soldiers who served in the military or naval or air service and were discharged, or are no longer part of active duty

Index

Websites to Visit

https://kids.kiddle.co/Service_animal

https://easyscienceforkids.com/all-about-guide-and-service-dogs/

https://www.kidzworld.com/article/24593-all-about-assistance-dogs/

About the Author

B. Keith Davidson

B. Keith Davidson grew up around dogs and has always been fascinated by the bonds that humans and these very special creatures share. Beagles are his favorite dogs, even if they are stubborn and frustrating. He has a Master's degree in Canadian History from Carleton University.

Written by: B. Keith Davidson
Designed by: Jennifer Dydyk
Edited by: Kelli Hicks
Proofreader: Janine Deschenes

Photographs: Cover illustration of Dog(also on title page) © Nevada3, photo of dog © Jose Luis Stephens, woman © Pixel-Shot, Page 4 Golden retriever © parsobchai Ngammoa, inset photo © MintImages, Page 5 top photo © Africa Studio, Great Dane © ButtermilkgirlVirginia, chihuahua © Microfile.org, Page 7 top photo © Monkey Business Images, bottom photo © Shine Caramia, Page 8 © SasaStock, Pages 9 and 10 © Africa Studio, Page 11 top photo © Cari Rubin Photography, bottom photo © Tim photo-video, Page 12 © Akimov Igor, Page 13 top photo © SasaStock, bottom photo © Pixel-Shot, Page 14 © r.classen, Page 15 dog © Pop Paul-Catalin, alarm © Dzm1try, Page 16 © ButtermilkgirlVirginia, Page 17 top photo © Jose Luis Stephens, bottom photo © Belish, Page 18 © WilleeCole Photography, Page 19 peanuts © Euripides, dog © BublikHaus, Page 20 top photo © aerophoto, bottom photo © GingerKitten, Page 21 © Igor Normann, Page 22 © Nina Buday, Page 23 top photo © GrungyBit, bottom photo © goodbishop, Page 24 © Belish, Page 25 top photo © IDN, bottom photo © Belish, Page 26 © PEPPERSMINT, Page 27 top photo © Trong Nguyen, bottom photo © ja-images, Page 28 top photo © Clare Louise Jackson, bottom photo © Big Bambi Productions, Page 29 top photo © Vitaly Titov, bottom photo © Africa Studio. All images from Shutterstock.com except page 6 © David Walsen https://creativecommons.org/licenses/by-sa/3.0/deed.en

Library and Archives Canada Cataloguing in Publication

CIP available at Library and Archives Canada

Library of Congress Cataloging-in-Publication Data

CIP available at Library of Congress

Crabtree Publishing Company

www.crabtreebooks.com 1-800-387-7650

 Printed in the U.S.A./CG20210915/012022

 In Canada: We acknowledge the financial support of the Government of Canada through the Canada Book Fund for our publishing activities.

Published in the United States
Crabtree Publishing
347 Fifth Avenue, Suite 1402-145
New York, NY, 10016

Published in Canada
Crabtree Publishing
616 Welland Ave.
St. Catharines, Ontario L2M 5V6